RACISM AND THE CHURCH

Dr. Ronald A. James, DD

Unless otherwise indicated, the Scriptures quoted are taken from the Authorized King James Version of the Bible. NIV denotes New International Version.

RACISM AND THE CHURCH
Dr. Ronald A. James, DD
Post Office Box 957996
Duluth, Georgia 30095

ISBN 978-1-943342-57-0

Designed and Published by:
Heavenly Enterprises Midwest, Ltd.
Chicago, Illinois • 773-783-2981
service@heavenlyenterprises.com

Foreword

"For we wrestle not against flesh and blood, but against powers and principalities and rulers of wickedness in high places." Ephesians 6:12

Spiritual warfare is real. Aware or unaware we encounter forces of evil whose goal it is to discourage, defeat and divide. The principality of racism is deep rooted in America's structure. Many will say that we need to "fix our system." The system isn't broken—it is functioning just as oppressively as it was intended to function! We need a new system—a new structure. However, if the new structure has the same roots it will essentially be the same system. Dismantling racism is a hot button topic in today's societal climate. Spiritually we can understand dismantling racism as dealing with the layers of demonic activity attacking humankind. Essentially, creating a new system.

The Church ought to be the one place where Christians can go for safety from the evil of this world. However, since the Church as we know it was built within an oppressive system it struggles with the ability to be the source of comfort and empowerment for all who are weary and worn. The moral authority of the Church has declined as Pastors build mini-empires unto themselves and the church members become their subjects. Week after week from pulpits all across this land men and women preach a gospel of fluff. The prophetic edge has been diminished as we have entered full throttle into the age of prosperity and individuality.

While folks are busy getting our blessings the forces of darkness are having a hey-day. The principality of racism manifests itself in hatred, disparities, injustices, inequities, trauma and death of body and spirit. The body of Christ must wake up and join in community to raise our voices in protest against the evil one. Turning a blind eye to the effects of racism within our places of worship is no longer acceptable.

Soldiers are being summoned to take up arms (the weapons of this warfare are not carnal but mighty through God for the pulling down of strongholds—2 Corinthians 10:4). We are being commissioned onto the battlefield. Every wise soldier knows that they must be trained before going to battle. It is our responsibility to learn everything we can about the enemy we are fighting. We must be able to identify it by its works and effects within ourselves and then to our broader communities.

Dr. Ronald James has penned a powerful educational tool for those seeking to understand the activity of the spiritual realm. This book is a light in the darkness of our present day. As you read these words you will be compelled to respond. Respond first with self-examination, confession, repentance and repair. Afterwards, be a repairer of the breech in your community. Rise and speak truth to power. Fast and pray. Bind and loose.

Above all, love—love is THE undefeatable force in this universe. Love never fails because God is love. Love will cause us to see ourselves in the "other." Love will cause us to seek out good for the sake of good. Through love we will witness the walls of racism crumble. The Church militant will be the Church triumphant because #LoveAlwaysWins!

~ Reverend Renita Marie Green, M.Div.
Ferguson, Missouri

Table of Contents

Racism and the Church

Introduction

First of all, I want to make it very clear that this book is not written with the purpose of pointing the finger or placing the blame, guilt or shame on any specific ethnic group. Racism has been used to inflict atrocities on certain ethnic groups by other ethnic groups from Africa, Europe, Asia and South America. My hope is to expose this principality and power of racism that has divided the Body of Christ for centuries and expose its tactics.

In order to recognize the symptoms and signs of racism and to formulate the correct strategies in defeating racism, we must diligently explore, in depth, the results and effects of racism within the body of Christ. Biblical history is our best teacher. This includes history recorded in the Bible and recent history recorded in the modern church.

If we believe that the Bible is relevant for this and every generation, then we should not be surprised to discover that there are many accounts of racism within the Holy Scriptures. It should also not be surprising that the answers in how God by His Spirit, deals with and defeats this principality and power, are held within its pages.

My goal for this text is to heighten the believers' awareness of racism, race and ethnic issues that have been ignored for quite some time in order for us to understand how The God of heaven and earth views all of His people. I hope that this will help the entire Body of Christ, regardless of ethnicity, culture, or background, to understand their unique role in the last day glory of the Church that Jesus Christ is building.

Although racism is prevalent throughout all aspects of modern society in America and throughout the world and has affected most institutions and governmental structures, I will be focusing primarily on how racism has and is still opposing God's plan for the earth and His kingdom. Racism is not just a black-white problem; it is a worldwide, multi-national spiritually demonic entity that continues to oppose God and bring division to the body of Christ. This book will discuss terms that are critical to the conversation surrounding race in the church, focus on specific events in both biblical and American church history that have defined Christianity and the battle for race relations today, as well as offer suggestions toward race healing for "all" of the Body of Christ

CHAPTER 1

Who Determines All?

Galatians 2:28 "There is neither Jew nor Greek, there is neither bond nor free, there is neither male nor female: for ye are all one in Christ Jesus."

"Christ not only died for all: He died for each."
— Billy Graham

In the Old Testament, Joel 2:28-29, the Prophet Joel spoke the word of God, obviously teaching to the fullness of mankind, the seed of Adam. Joel prophesied,

*"And it shall come to pass afterward, that I will pour out my spirit upon **all** flesh; and your sons and your daughters shall prophesy, your old men shall dream dreams, your young men shall see visions: And also upon the servants and upon the handmaids in those days will I pour out my spirit." (KJV bold added)*

In the New Testament, Acts 2:17-18, Peter reiterated

what was said by Joel, making a declaration that the prophetic word spoken by the Prophet Joel was being fulfilled: all of mankind would have the Spirit of God poured out upon them, regardless of ethnicity, social economic status or gender. Peter shared,

"And it shall come to pass in the last days, saith God, I will pour out of my Spirit upon **all** flesh: and your sons and your daughters shall prophesy, and your young men shall see visions, and your old men shall dream dreams: And on my servants and on my handmaidens I will pour out in those days of my Spirit; and they shall prophesy…"

According to both the Hebrew and the Greek, the word "all" excludes no one, for any reason:

All
Hebrew
kôl kôl
kole, kole
From H3634; properly the *whole*; hence *all, any* or *every* (in the singular only, but often in a plural sense): - (in) all (manner, [ye]), altogether, any (manner), enough, every (one, place, thing), howsoever, as many as, [no-] thing, ought, whatsoever, (the) whole, whoso (-ever).

All
Greek
pas
pas
Including all the forms of declension; apparently a primary word; *all, any, every,* the *whole:* - all (manner of, means) alway (-s), any (one), X daily, + ever, every (one, way), as many as, + no (-thing), X throughly,

whatsoever, whole, whosoever.

In these definitions, the word "all" is inclusive of everyone; however, this may not be what some believe "all" is meant to be! During the formative stages of our nation, Africans and their descendants were not considered 100% human. Even the Native Americans, who first inhabited the Americas before any other ethnic group, were viewed as savages and treated as nuisances, much like coyotes or other vermin. Given this definition of "all," what, then, allowed believers in Jesus Christ to justify the inhumane treatment of Africans, Native Americans and others ethnicities? There must be a reason.

Before we can comprehend the depths of what racism is and more, how it has affected the Church, we should distinguish between "racism" and other terms that may be associated with this conversation.

Prejudice

The word prejudice refers to prejudgment: i.e. making a decision before becoming aware of the relevant facts of a case. In recent times, the word has come to be most often used to refer to preconceived, usually unfavorable, judgments toward people or a person because of gender, social class, age, disability, religion, sexuality, race/ethnicity, language, nationality or other personal characteristics. In this case, it refers to a positive or negative evaluation of another person based on his or her group membership.[1] Prejudice can also refer to unfounded beliefs[2] and may include, "any unreasonable attitude that is unusually resistant to rational influence."[3] Gordon Allport defined prejudice as a "feeling, favorable or unfavorable, toward a person

3

or thing, prior to, or not based on, actual experience."[4] (*Prejudice*)

Discrimination

Discrimination is the prejudicial and/or distinguishing treatment of an individual based on their actual or perceived membership in a certain group or category, "in a way that is worse than the way people are usually treated."[1] It involves the group's initial reaction or interaction, influencing the individual's actual <u>behavior</u> towards the group or the group leader, restricting members of one group from opportunities or privileges that are available to another group, leading to the exclusion of the individual or entities based on logical or irrational decision-making.[2] (*Discrimination*)

Racism

And finally, here are several definitions of racism: "A belief that race is the primary determinant of human traits and capacities and that racial differences produce an inherent superiority of a particular race." (*Racism*, Merriam-Webster)

"Racism is usually defined as views, practices and actions reflecting the belief that humanity is divided into distinct biological groups called races and that members of a certain race share certain attributes which make that group as a whole less desirable, more desirable, inferior or superior." (*Racism*, Wikipedia)

"A belief that all members of each race possess characteristics, abilities, or qualities specific to that race, especially so as to distinguish it as inferior or superior to another race or races." (*Racism*, Oxford)

In 1970, the U.S. Commission of Civil Rights coined the name racism, "Any attitude, action or institutional structure which subordinates a person or group because of their color . . . Racism is not just a matter of attitudes; actions and institutional structures can also be a form of racism." (*Definitions of Racism*)

Dr. Delmo Della Dora, former professor at California State University and race advocate stated, "Racism is different from racial prejudice, hatred, or discrimination. Racism involves having the power to carry out systematic discriminatory practices through the major institutions of our society." (*Definitions of Racism*)

For my purposes in this book, I have a very simple definition: **Racism is prejudice with power**, and the concept of "All" is distorted many ethnic groups may have negative opinions and views about each other; the problem comes when you have the power to enforce and implement those views into actions, and then create institutions to both enforce and reinforce those beliefs, regardless of whether the beliefs are accurate or inaccurate.

Racism is not only a belief that a particular ethnic group is better than another it is a principality. What this principality of racism does is give a specific ethnic group in power, not only the justification or the moral right, but the ability to create and sustain this mindset within its group and designs institutional structures that benefit, perpetuate and solidify the dominant groups with the power. These groups use media, social programs and health care organizations such as Planned Parenthood, with its practices of eugenics, police forces, educational systems, and unfortunately, even the Church reinforcing this spirit, keeping the dominant group in power.

> *"For we wrestle not against flesh and blood, but against principalities, against powers, against the rulers of the darkness of this world, against spiritual wickedness in high places." (KJV Ephesians 6:12)*

Principality
noun, plural principalities.

1. a state ruled by a prince, usually a relatively small state or a state that falls within a larger state such as a empire.
2. the position or authority of a prince or chief ruler; sovereignty; supreme power.
3. the rule of a prince of a small or subordinate state.
4. the Principality, British.
5. principalities, Theology.
   a. an order of angles.
   b. supra-mundane powers often in conflict with God. Ephes. 6:12.

Source - Random House, Inc. (2016). dictionary.com Unabridged

Racism also tries to convince the oppressed ethnic group that they are not equal to the dominant ethnic group, thereby justifying the oppression. It is important to know that racism is a principality that, if left unchecked, will ultimately lead to genocide!

> *John 10:10 "The thief cometh not, but for to steal, and to kill, and to destroy: I am come that*

they might have life, and that they might have it more abundantly."

We have witnessed this principality in recent history on a national scale in Rwanda in 1994 where over 500,000 Hutu and Tutsi were killed. Both were tribes that reside within Rwanda!

As John 10:10 states, the ultimate goal of all demonic principalities, including racism, is to steal, kill and destroy. When we see one ethnic group stealing from, killing and then destroying everything another ethnic group has taken years, even generations to build, it is a sure sign that the principality of racism is fully manifesting itself. However, we must remember the concept of "All":

> *Galatians 3:26-28 "For ye are* **all** *the children of God by faith in Christ Jesus. For* **as many of you** *as have been baptized into Christ have put on Christ. There is neither Jew nor Greek, there is neither bond nor free, there is neither male nor female: for ye are* **all one** *in Christ Jesus." (KJV bold added)*

In the book of Galatians, Chapter 3 the Apostle Paul explains that once we become Christ's, we are one, or equal:

Equal access to God,
Equal worth to God,
Equal anointing in God.
Equal authority in God.
Equal in all aspect that pertain to the things of God.

This scripture specifically addresses that being a

bondman or woman (slave) did not make you a lesser or second class Christian. Slaves or servants were not uncommon during Old Testament or New Testament times, yet the writers of these verses were led by the Holy Spirit to make it clear that the position of one's servitude did not exclude him or her from the "All."

Unaware/Unintentional/Subversive Racism

Another aspect of racism that we will explore is unaware/unintentional/subversive racism. These adjectives address the circumstance that occurs when members of the dominant culture are not aware that they have racist tendencies. Many of the dominant culture in this category have good intentions, and are appalled by acts and ideas of overt racism and can identify it when they see it, but they have difficulty recognizing behaviors within themselves that are racist. This form of racism is the most difficult to defeat because the person, church or group does not believe themselves to be racist and will resist efforts to address their own acts of racism, often dismissing them as coincidence or simply acts of bad judgment.

As Christians, those who follow the teaching of the Bible, our ethnicity, although important is not primary; as Galatians 3 has indicated, we are neither Jew, Greek, white, black, yellow, red or brown; our induction into the family of God is the point. Therefore, if one felt that the argument of the curse of Ham, or any other ethnic argument would cause people of dark skin to be destined to slavery, or cause people of a different ethnicity to be inferior, this belief is not supported by the Bible.

Galatians 3:26-28 is clear that regardless of ethnicity, gender, class, slave or free, our status as children in the kingdom of God are equal; there are no grandchildren, stepchildren, nieces or nephews but we are **all one**. Unfortunately, racism will cause a reader of the Bible to ignore these verses and allow cultural and societal norms to be accepted, believed and taught.

If that is not enough biblical evidence Galatians 3:13 should make it clear.

> *Galatians 3:13-14 "Christ hath redeemed us from the curse of the law, being made a curse for us: for it is written, Cursed is every one that hangeth on a tree: that the blessing of Abraham might come on the Gentiles through Jesus Christ; that we might receive the promise of the Spirit through faith."*

Racism is a principality and power that is connected with pride and deception; therefore, biblical concepts that may seem obvious to some may be impossible to believe or understand unless the power and influence of this principality is broken. The Apostle Peter is an example of that. Even after the day of Pentecost, Peter had difficulty understanding and receiving God's plan that all ethnicities were one in Christ. Although all ethnicities heard the word of the Lord in their own language, Peter still had difficulty. God himself was giving Peter visions of His plan to include every ethnicity. The Jewish tradition and Peter's training about the Jews being God's chosen people made it almost impossible for him to believe that God would make all the Gentiles equal to the Jews in their relationship with God.

Peter was dealing with an issue of pride. Obadiah 1:3 states that, "The pride of thine heart hath deceived thee, thou that dwellest in the clefts of the rock, whose habitation *is* high; that saith in his heart, Who shall bring me down to the ground?"

The demonic realm affects the unsaved and the saved, yet only the saved, by the power of God, can be made free from its influence. I say made free because all of us, white, black, brown, red and yellow, have been affected by this principality. Whether it has touched us directly or we have felt the effect from generations of injustice or privilege, racism has stolen, killed, and destroyed multitudes of people, polluting the minds of well-meaning Christians to keep the body of Christ divided.

In most dominant cultures, dominance has been gained by oppressing other cultures through forceful, financial, and or psychological means. In the body of Christ, there must be ministry and prayer in order for all cultures involved to break free of this spirit and the stereotypes it produces.

White Privilege

White privilege (or **white skin privilege**) plays a role in the discussion of "All,' as well. It refers to the set of societal privileges that white people are argued to benefit from beyond those commonly experienced by people of color in the same social, political, or economic spaces (nation, community, workplace, income, etc.). The term denotes both obvious and less obvious, spoken and unspoken advantages that white individuals may not recognize they have, which distinguishes it from overt bias or prejudice. These include cultural affirmations of one's own worth; presumed greater social status; and freedom to move, buy, work, play, and speak freely. The concept of white privilege also implies the right to assume the universality of one's own experiences, marking others as different or exceptional while perceiving oneself as normal. It can be compared and/or combined with the concept of male privilege. (*Male Privilege*)

This privilege also extends into the body of Christ. When I first became a follower of Jesus Christ, I assumed that what the Bible says about His sons and daughters being brothers and sisters would create an equality of people and ethnicities that I had not experienced prior to my conversion. I was wrong! I believed that God had placed my family in an area whose population was predominantly of European decent, but even in Christ, I was keenly aware that I was not thought of or treated as an equal with the other pastors who were all of European decent.

Even though I have been a leader all my life: captain on my high school and college wrestling teams, Junior Achievement, leader of a secular band that traveled throughout the world, overseeing networks of churches and more, if I was confident as a leader, or even as a strong man, it was considered pride, arrogance or aloofness. My revelation and understanding concerning biblical things was lesser and my ideas were not used unless the dominant European American pastors believed it was first their idea.

In a town where there is little diversity, which is located in a state and country where people of color are actually present, the lack of people of color in the ministry or leadership of ministries should be an obvious sign that the principality of racism is in operation.

Professor James M. Jones postulates three major types of racism:
(i) Personally-mediated, (ii) internalized, and (iii) institutionalized. Personally-mediated racism includes the specific social attitudes inherent to racially-prejudiced action (bigoted differential assumptions about abilities, motives, and the intentions of others according to, discrimination (the differential actions and behaviors towards others according to their race) stereotyping, commission, and omission (disrespect, suspicion, devaluation, and dehumanization). Internalized racism is the acceptance, by members of the racially-stigmatized people of negative perceptions about their own abilities and intrinsic worth, characterized by low self-esteem and low esteem of others like them. This racism can be manifested through embracing "whiteness" (e.g. stratification by skin color in non-white communities), self-devaluation (e.g. racial slurs, nicknames, rejection of ancestral culture, etc.) and resignation, helplessness, and hopelessness (e.g. dropping out of school, failing to vote, engaging in health-risk practices, etc.). (*Institutionalized Racism*)

When this institutionalized racist spirit is entrenched within the church, doctrine, rules, bylaws are constructed around racist tendencies, both overt and unaware. Making it even more difficult to pull down the spirit due to major changes in the structural makeup of the institutions within the church. This is when the spirit of racism, working together with fear, begins to do everything it can to tighten its hold of all that has been gained through its dominance over other cultures. Change will require release of power, authority and even resources.

It begins with the spirit within as in Exodus 5:15-16:

> *"Then the officers of the children of Israel came and cried unto Pharaoh, saying, Wherefore dealest thou thus with thy servants? There is no straw given unto thy servants, and they say to us, Make brick: and, behold, thy servants are beaten; but the fault is in thine own people."*

If left unchecked, it eventually becomes a stronghold:

> *2 Corinthians 10:4-6 "For the weapons of our warfare are not carnal, but mighty through God to the pulling down of strong holds; Casting down imaginations, and **every** high thing that exalteth itself against the knowledge of God, and bringing into captivity every thought to the obedience of Christ; and having in a readiness to revenge all disobedience, when your obedience is fulfilled." (KJV bold added)*

But there is hope because the Bible reminds us in II Corinthians 5:17, "Therefore if any man *be* in Christ, *he is* a new creature: old things are passed away; behold, all things are become new."

CHAPTER 2

History of Racism in the Church/Bible

"There is not even a common language when the term 'equity' is used. Negro and white have a fundamentally different definition. Negros have proceeded from a premise that equality means what it says... But most whites in America ... Proceed from a premise that equality is a loose expression for improvement. White America is not even psychologically organized to close the gap-essentially it seeks only to retain it."
— *Rev. Dr. Martin Luther King Jr.*

Like most demonic efforts, racism is not a new occurrence. One of the more prominent instances is in Numbers 12:1 when Miriam and Aaron spoke against Moses and his Ethiopian wife. This is an early example of Jews/Hebrews who have married people of African descent. Just for your information, in case you did not know, Egypt and Ethiopia are in Africa! Pride blinds well-intending Christians to very evident, geographical facts about people and places in the Bible.

This frequently causes the dominant ethnic group to ignore obvious references to people and places of color in the scriptures.

If we truly understand that Jehovah God choose Abram out of a Gentile or heathen nation, then we can comprehend the plan of God to bring all ethnicities together into one Kingdom. Many of the Jews/Hebrews married outside of their ethnicity, yet God welcomed them as long as they forsook their pagan gods and pledged their belief in Jehovah.

Racism in the church has evolved into not just a belief that the dominant ethnic group, Europeans and European Americans, are inherently better that others, but has transferred them into "the chosen people." God favors them because God has blessed their ministries. This belief is institutionalized racism: the entire structure is infiltrated with this principality of racism, promoting one ethnic group over another. At first glance, it might seem as though this only permeates American culture, but a closer look at the church and at its practices as a whole over centuries would indicate otherwise.

I will use many secular references and studies since the church, with all of its resources, has done little to study this ever-growing impasse to the Kingdom. Although acts of racism are recorded throughout the Old and New Testament, this is not the will of God nor is it validated in the New Testament.

The Day of Pentecost

Acts 2:16-18 "But this is that which was spoken by the prophet Joel; And it shall come to pass in the last days, saith God, I will pour out of my Spirit upon all flesh: and your sons and your daughters shall prophesy, and your young men shall see visions, and your old men shall dream dreams: And on my servants and on my handmaidens I will pour out in those days of my Spirit; and they shall prophesy."

Joel 2:28-29 "And it shall come to pass afterward, that I will pour out my spirit upon all flesh; and your sons and your daughters shall prophesy, your old men shall dream dreams, your young men shall see visions: And also upon the servants and upon the handmaids in those days will I pour out my spirit."

These two sections of scripture, one Old Testament and one New Testament, have been used by the Charismatic and Pentecostal movements to validate being filled with the Spirit, and rightly so. Unfortunately, some have missed the fact that "all flesh" means that ethnicity will not be a factor when God determines upon whom to place His Spirit or who He would use to fulfill His Divine Plans. Even if you were a slave or servant, God's Spirit would not skip you. Everyone has the same Holy Spirit, which means God values everyone equally.

During the first century church, although the prophet Joel had prophesied that it would happen, many Jews were surprised and even shocked to see that God's Spirit fell on Gentiles as it had fallen on them on the day of Pentecost, giving Gentiles equal standing in the Kingdom of God. This was especially difficult to understand and accept after centuries of being, "God's chosen people."

This is the same reason that some, not all, European Americans find it difficult to believe and understand that God does and will use people of any color in all aspects of His Kingdom. Unfortunately, being the dominant culture in America for over two centuries has caused many to believe that God favors them and not other ethnicities.

During the time of Pentecost, Rome was a center for power and authority, even in Jerusalem. It is amazing if you study the role that the Romans played in Christ's Crucifixion as well as their role in the inclusion of doctrines that were not those of the Apostles. Roman citizenship was used as a tool of foreign policy and control. Colonies and political allies would be granted a "minor" form of Roman citizenship. The promise of improved standing within the Roman "sphere of influence" and the rivalry for standing with one's neighbors kept many of Rome's neighbors from trying to subvert or overthrow Rome's influence.

Jesus and the Samaritan Woman

The account in John, chapter 4 of the Samaritan woman at the well is a prime example of Jesus Christ extending salvation to the Gentiles, non-Jews.

> John 4:7-9 "There cometh a woman of Samaria to draw water: Jesus saith unto her, Give me to drink. (For his disciples were gone away unto the city to buy meat.) Then saith the woman of Samaria unto him, How is it that thou, being a Jew, askest drink of me, which am a woman of Samaria? for the Jews have no dealings with the Samaritans."

This woman understood that Jews had very little to do with Samaritans and was both shocked and surprised that Jesus, a Jew, asked her for a drink. This shows the negative impact that racism had on the woman, who might not have dialoged with the Savior and missed her time of visitation if she had adhered to the societal norms. Fortunately, she pressed in and the entire city was able to receive Jesus Christ. Jesus, the Christ, however, had to send the disciples away in order to minister to this woman. Even upon their return, they questioned in their hearts the nature of Jesus' conversation with her, a Samaritan.

> *John 4:27 "And upon this came his disciples, and marvelled that he talked with the woman: yet no man said, What seekest thou? or, Why talkest thou with her?"*

Many times, the oppressed ethnic group has two primary responses: 1. of withdrawal, in order to have as little interaction with the dominant ethnic group as possible and be subjected to as little oppression as possible, and/or 2. of hostility and defiance, openly opposing the dominant ethnic group. Of course, there are varying degrees and methods that each individual might apply to achieve this, but some type of response will surely come. Fortunately for the Woman at the Well, she had neither response, and she was able to receive the Salvation of Jesus.

The Council at Jerusalem

> *Acts 15:7-10 "And when there had been much disputing, Peter rose up, and said unto them, Men and brethren, ye know how that a good while ago God made choice among us, that the*

Gentiles by my mouth should hear the word of the gospel, and believe. And God, which knoweth the hearts, bare them witness, giving them the Holy Ghost, even as he did unto us; And put **no difference between us and them***, purifying their hearts by faith. Now therefore why tempt ye God, to put a yoke upon the neck of the disciples, which neither our fathers nor we were able to bear?" (KJV bold added)*

After this gathering, the remaining apostles wrote letters in regards to the fact that Gentiles, along with their ethnic backgrounds, were accepted by God and the New Testament leaders.

Peter, the same apostle that received the revelation of Jesus Christ being the Son of God, began to understand that all who come into the Kingdom of God have equal standing. If we refuse to acknowledge this plain and this simple fact, as Peter did initially, we too are in danger of tempting God Himself.

Some of the same Pentecostal/Charismatic denominations who use these scriptures are the most racist in the body of Christ. As the disciples were in danger of carrying such a yoke, the yoke that is put upon people of color is assimilation! Peter and the true Israelites/Hebrews would never assimilate to other cultures. Even in the midst of captivity Daniel, Joseph, and many others refused to assimilate, even if it meant prison or death.

Now, cultural assimilation is the process whereby a minority group gradually adapts to the customs and attitudes of the prevailing culture and customs. (*Cultural Assimilation*) Often, in order to be successful within an environment where racism exists, the dominated culture may be deceived into thinking that cultural assimilation will cause them to be accepted. Unfortunately, a culture of racism will never fully accept another culture! To be a follower of Jesus Christ, you did not need to become a Jew first. In the first paragraph top of page switch the words; people to places and places to people. What I needed to do as a Gentile, according to Acts 15:20, was abstain from idols, and from fornication or sexual impurity, food that was strangled, and blood. Any culture could adhere to this; the Apostles recognized this and the spirit of racism was defeated. They were able to do this regardless of the entrenched and strengthened spirit that had grown over the centuries by some well-meaning, and some not so well-meaning, followers of Christ.

The Curse of Ham

Some scholars, Bible teachers and church leaders have attributed the woes of dark skinned people, including slavery, mistreatment and servitude to the curse of Ham, son of Noah.

> *Genesis 9:20-25 And Noah began to be an husbandman, and he planted a vineyard: And he drank of the wine, and was drunken; and he was uncovered within his tent. And Ham, the father of Canaan, saw the nakedness of his father, and told his two brethren without. And Shem and Japheth took a garment, and laid it upon both their shoulders, and went backward, and covered the nakedness of their father; and their faces were backward, and they saw not their father's nakedness. And Noah awoke*

*from his wine, and knew what his younger son
had done unto him. And he said, Cursed be
Canaan; a servant of servants shall he be unto
his brethren."*

Some have even justified their overt racism because of
this passage; however, slavery for African Americans
is an American issue. Common sense would tell you
that the curse would not skip thousands of years and
start in the 20th Century. This demonic spirit causes
intelligent people to ignore obvious facts.

Rahab, mentioned in the genealogy of Jesus Christ in
Mathew 1, was a Canaanite. A descendant of Ham, she
must have married an Israelite in order to appear in this
genealogy. Since this was a marriage approved by God,
it shows that the particular "race" she came from was
not important; it matters only that she trusted in the
true God of Israel. Ruth, a Moabite, was also featured
in the genealogy of Jesus Christ. She expressed faith in
the true God before her marriage to Boaz. (Ruth 1-16)
According to author Ken Ham, "The only marriages
that God warns against are God's people marrying
unbelievers."[1]

Regarding slavery, many races have been enslaved; even
the Jews in their history were slaves in Egypt for several
hundred years. It would be difficult to specify when
the transition happened from Joseph and free Jews/
Hebrews to slavery. Slavery even had a long history in
the ancient world and was practiced in Ancient Egypt
and Greece, as well as in Rome. Most slaves during the
Roman Empire were foreigners and, unlike in modern
times, Roman slavery was not based on race but on
Roman citizenship. Slaves in Rome might include
prisoners of war, sailors captured and sold by pirates,

or slaves purchased outside Roman territory. In hard times, it was not uncommon for desperate Roman citizens to raise money by selling their children into slavery.

While there were all sorts of rationale for slavery, the Apostle Paul taught in Galatians 3:13-14, "Christ hath redeemed us from the curse of the law, being made a curse for us: for it is written, Cursed *is* every one that hangeth on a tree: That the blessing of Abraham might come on the Gentiles through Jesus Christ; that we might receive the promise of the Spirit through faith."

Regardless of this scriptural support, by the 19th century, many Bible historians agreed that Africans' and African Americans' lineage from Ham was a primary justification for slavery among Southern Christians. Ham was indeed Noah's descendant, but if we believe the Bible that Noah and his sons restarted the human race after the flood, and ultimately all nations of the earth, Ham was as much a part of that recreation as his brothers were. He and his brothers came from the same gene pool. The spirit of racism that drives these beliefs will cause you to skew the facts, ignore logic and, if not careful, develop doctrines of devils!

Even so, if there was a curse that was issued on the descendants of Ham, this scripture should nullify or redeem that group of people and his descendants. Amazingly, many Bible scholars did not believe that Christ's blood did enough or that His death, burial and resurrection were enough to break even this curse of Ham over his descendants. Because of the lack of deliverance ministries, and the casting out of devils, many Evangelicals and Pentecostals have little understanding about breaking curses. Regardless, any curse, including the so-called curse of Ham, is easily broken by the sacrifice that Christ made at Calvary.

It is often taught that America was built on Christian principles, yet in an effort to justify slavery and the mistreatment of other human beings, African Americans were constitutionally counted as only 3/5 human. American Christians and slave owners willingly ascribed to this accounting system created by the government, ultimately, so that the southern states would not have control in Congress.

Although there is a history of racism in both the Bible and in human history, the Bible has a history of inclusion and acceptance of all ethnicities while defeating racism because of the blood of Jesus.

Ruth

Ruth 1:4 "And they took them wives of the women of Moab; the name of the one was Orpah, and the name of the other Ruth: and they dwelled there about ten years."

The Moabites, Ruth's ethnic group, are described as descendants of Lot's son, Moab

Ruth 4:17 "And the women her neighbours gave it a name, saying, There is a son born to Naomi; and they called his name Obed: he is the father of Jesse, the father of David."

The Azusa Street Revival

The contemporary struggle of racism in the church was still alive and well in 1905, as the seeds of racism born in the early church spread easily to the American church. At that time, William Seymour, a young, African American preacher, had learned of a new, groundbreaking religious theology called Pentecostalism, being taught by Charles Parham. Parham served the Methodist Episcopal Church as a supply pastor (he was never ordained) in Topeka, Kansas. Seymour requested and received a license as a minister of Parham's Apostolic Faith Movement, and he initially considered his work in Los Angeles under Parham's authority. However, Seymour soon broke with Parham over his harsh criticism of the emotional worship at Azusa Street and the intermingling of whites and blacks in the services. (*Charles Fox Parham*)

Because of the strict segregation laws of the times, Seymour was forced to sit outside of the meeting room during the training that Parham did on the Holy Spirit, yet the humble servant of God bore the injustice with grace. Parham and Seymour held joint meetings in Houston, with Seymour preaching to black audiences and Parham speaking to the white audiences. Parham hoped to use Seymour to spread the Apostolic Faith message to the African Americans in Texas.

According to author Tony Cauchi in his article, *William Seymour and the History of the Azusa Street Outpouring,*

> In the beginning, these meetings were attended mainly by "Negro washwomen," and a few of their husbands. Despite the lack of personal experience of the 'baptism' with the 'Bible evidence' of speaking with tongues and the apparent lack of results in his hearers, Seymour ploughed on in faith and assurance that the blessing was on its way.
>
> Other local church pastors heard about the holiness preacher who was preaching and expecting the next "move of God." Gradually, certainly by late March 1906, these white believers had joined the little group of African-Americans at the house on Bonnie Brae Street and were actively seeking the baptism with the Holy Spirit as evidenced by speaking with other tongues.[3]

The Azusa Street Revival, led by Seymour in Los Angeles, was a mixture of the White American Holiness religion and the worship derived from the African American Christian tradition. The worship and praise at Azusa Street used a style that came from the Appalachian Whites and Southern Blacks and included dancing and shouting. This merging of Black and White, men and women and the participation from all of the ethnic minorities of Los Angeles was a phenomenon that was almost unheard of in 1906. It has been described as the "color line being washed away in the Blood." William Seymour became the most influential black leader and is credited as being the co-founder, along with Charles Parham, of the world of Pentecostalism. Many European Americans refuse to even acknowledge Seymour's contribution to the movement, even though his ministry is the one that had documented manifestation of the Holy Spirit.

The Emancipation Proclamation would be issued by President Abraham Lincoln on January 1, 1863 as a measure to declare all slaves free, but even this legislation did not help Seymour over 40 years later. The racism that Seymour endured at the hand of whites, particularly Charles Parham, may have caused him to conclude that some people who claimed salvation might not really have had Christ in their hearts. Interestingly enough, it has been historically noted that Charles Parham was a racist, becoming a full-fledged member of the KKK by 1910. I believe they both just needed a revelation of deliverance, a casting out of devils.

According to a witness, Frank Bartleman, the meetings were like no other:

> Divine love was wonderfully manifest in the meetings. They would not even allow an unkind word said against their opposers or the churches. The message was 'the love of God.' It was a sort of 'first love' of the early church returned. The 'baptism,' as we received it in the beginning, did not allow us to think, speak or hear evil of any man. The Spirit was very sensitive, tender as a dove.
> Los Angeles Times, April 18, 1906

Despite all of the documented manifestations of the Holy Spirit, Charles Parham, insulted by the racial make-up of the meetings, specifically the mix of men of color with white women, brought the first church split.

William H. Durham: One European American pastor from Chicago who did not allow color or race to stop him from receiving was William H. Durham. After attending an Azusa Street meeting, being filled with the Holy Spirit and receiving a prophecy from William Seymour, he began to teach and preach with many of the same signs and wonders that were apparent at Azusa Street.

Cecil M. Robeck, Jr., Ph.D. of Pasadena, California taught in his article, *A Pentecostal Perspective on Leadership,*

> The inclusive, egalitarian character of Seymour's leadership style suggests that Seymour's personality was well suited for ministry to those he led at the Mission. They were one of the most racially inclusive, culturally diverse groups to gather in the city of Los Angeles at that time. The mission included people from many classes, male and female, black, white, Hispanic and Asian, the highly educated and the illiterate, new converts, and highly trained longtime professionals in ministry.[2]

The integrated worship of Azusa Street did not last long past the Revival itself. The African Americans organized under the Church of God in Christ and the European American Pentecostals congregated as the

Assemblies of God denominations, both coming from the Azusa Street Revival, yet not worshipping together.

Today, the Methodist Church largely dismisses what Parham taught and what Seymour demonstrated. When you inspect the majority of the denominational churches today, segregation and separation of ethnic cultures is the norm.

Revelation

Even though Seymour had great diversity within his leadership (I want to make it clear that Seymour not only had diversity in his followers but the leadership of Azusa Street Church also), his ethnicity caused many Europeans and European Americans to reject the revelation of the "Holy Spirit" which had been documented and validated by God with signs and wonders; the infilling of the Holy Spirit was still in question. After over 100 years of Spirit-filled activity, there are still denominations that refuse to receive this revelation of the "Holy Spirit", yet Mark 16:20 says, "And they went forth, and preached everywhere, the Lord working with *them,* and confirming the word with signs following. Amen."

Despite this scripture, this inability to receive new--or should I say revealed--understanding of scripture from people of color still permeates the body of Christ today.

One of the first significant church historians to recognize Seymour's importance was Sidney Ahlstrom, of Yale University. In 1972, he said that Seymour was "the most influential black leader in American religious history." The Assemblies of God Theological Seminary dedicated their new chapel to Seymour's memory in

1998. As the twentieth century closed, the Religion Newswriters Association named the Azusa Street Revival as one of the top ten events of the past millennium; *Life Magazine* **listed Azusa Street as one of the top one hundred events of the millennium; and,** *Christian History* **magazine named William J. Seymour one of the top ten Christians of the 20th century.**

Despite all of the success, the revival faced opposition from without and within. Charles Parham, insulted by the racial composition of the meetings and emotionalism brought the first major split. Many others followed. When Seymour married Miss Jeanne Evans Moore on May 13, 1908, another group left the mission.

Resources and Equality

Acts 6:1 "And in those days, when the number of the disciples was multiplied, there arose a murmuring of the Grecians against the Hebrews, because their widows were neglected in the daily ministration."

During the midst of the church being multiplied and an undeniable move of God, Greek widows were being neglected and disregarded; this caused the Greeks to murmur against the Hebrews. It appears that the resources were not being equally distributed among those widows in need.

> *Acts 2:44-47 And all that believed were together, and had all things common; And sold their possessions and goods, and parted them to all men, as every man had need and they, continuing daily with one accord in the temple, and breaking bread from house to house, did*

29

eat their meat with gladness and singleness of heart, Praising God, and having favour with all the people. And the Lord added to the church daily such as should be saved.

What happened from Acts, chapter 2 when all believers had "all things common" and "as every man had need" to a specific ethnic group being "neglected" of the daily resources in chapter 6? What caused there to be dissention between the Greeks and the Hebrews? What caused the Hebrews to neglect just the Greek widows?

It is important to note that one of the first attacks on the plan and move of God was racism! In subtle and cunning ways, it entered to undermine the unity of the faith and to cause God's people to actually believe that the racism was not devilish but a result of circumstances.

In Acts chapter 2:46, they were in one accord in the temple. The place of worship was united under the cause of God. In Acts 6:1, there was murmuring against the Hebrews, which made its way to the apostles. Even today, this principality is trying not only to distract the people but the apostolic leaders as well from their responsibility of study and prayer, severely hindering the move of God.

> *Acts 6:2 "Then the twelve called the multitude of the disciples unto them, and said, It is not reason that we should leave the word of God, and serve tables."*

The response by the apostles, "serve tables," may have had to do with the feeding or the daily rations that the

Greek widows should have been receiving. The fact that the writer of Acts and the Holy Spirit chose to make this ethnic distinction is important. The goal of this principality of racism was first to start murmuring and division among people, thereby stopping the move of God. The Hebrews were the group in power.

Second, the goal was to create an atmosphere of contention whereby the apostles would focus on this principality of racism instead of focusing on prayer and study of the Word.

> Acts 6:3 "Wherefore, brethren, look ye out among you seven men of honest report, full of the Holy Ghost and wisdom, whom we may appoint over this business."

The solution to defeating racism in this case was a joint effort with the apostles and the people. The affected people were allowed to work together with the dominant culture and solve the problem. Honesty comes first! We must be honest with ourselves in addressing the issues, not continually ignoring or neglecting obvious facts. In this situation, the dominant group was overlooking other ethnic groups, but including them is how we, as a church, can have a move of God. Often, however, many Christians of color are without the resources needed to do the work of the ministry.

Without the power of the Holy Ghost, it is impossible to defeat racism. I believe honesty is first because many have heard the Holy Spirit concerning racism but have not been honest or brave enough to do what the Holy Spirit has said. Going against friends and fellow members of your ethnic group or denomination takes bravery and trust in God.

Wisdom in how to implement what the Holy Spirit has said, but at the same time not offending anyone--which is difficult--and subsequently, getting everyone to recognize and stop any disparity between the ethnicities, is critical to making a change.

> *Acts 4:34-35 "Neither was there any among them that lacked: for as many as were possessors of lands or houses sold them, and brought the prices of the things that were sold, and laid them down at the apostles' feet: and distribution was made unto every man according as he had need."*

Obviously, there were people within the church who were in need. Today's theology is that if you are in the will of God, you will automatically be blessed with everything you need; therefore, there is no need to share resources with fellow churches within your community. It is more profitable to have missionary assignments to the poor in distant lands while neglecting those in need within your own community, especially if they are of a different ethnic group or denomination. How is it that a church or denomination can have a mission to Africa and Latin America but not help the African American and Latin American churches in their own communities?

The apostles had the wisdom of the Holy Spirit to distribute the resources to those who needed it, thereby keeping the entire body of Christ strong. The funds were not used to make an individual wealthy but to continue the work of the ministry.

In America, this lack of community has caused many leaders of color to separate themselves from

European Americans to create their own networks and financial institutions, while pooling resources amongst themselves. Many other leaders of color called by God, who happen to not be a part of these networks, will not be able to fulfill their destiny due to lack of resources.

The apostles who had a Kingdom outlook (See Luke 11:1-4) had more focus on the entirety of the Kingdom being made apparent on earth and not just on one ethnic group or one church with a cause. These men were able to distribute resources to those in need, regardless of their ethnicity.

Most Christian leaders of color in America, whether they are buying a building in which to worship, or purchasing a vehicle in which to pick up members, must go to European Americans, who are in power and authority in banks or mortgage companies, to obtain them. If the principality of racism is present, it will be impossible to succeed. Even when God calls particular ministries, the ministry still needs resources. If the dominant ethnic group has the power over the money, land, and resources, it will take honesty, the Holy Ghost, and wisdom to break through so that all ethnicities have the same access to provision, even if God is saying it.

Another sign of racism is broken or unrealized promises. Many who have recognized overt racism and have a desire to even the playing field have not been able to make much headway in this area. Often, this is because the people trying to make the adjustments are consumed with Unaware racism while others are not willing to confront all that it will take to defeat this principality. After the decree in Acts 15 that no other burdens should be placed on the Gentiles and, understanding that the Holy Spirit fell on the Gentiles as well as the Jewish believers it was made very clear. God promises to make no difference between them (Gentiles) and us (Jewish believers).

> Galatians 2:11 "But when Peter was come to Antioch, I withstood him to the face, because he was to be blamed."

In order for the promises to be fulfilled, Paul had to confront the Unaware racism deep within Peter in order for the decree to continue to be honored. Peter was there when this was decreed, yet he was still unable to do it! If his racism had been left unchecked, this decree would have been ignored and the gospel message hindered in Antioch.

Some brave people from the dominant group will need to step forward and confront many of the current day's leaders and say to them that they are to blame; in the Bible, the apostle Peter was rebuked for all generations to see. Just as racism can be blatant for all to see, the correction of racism cannot be done behind the scenes. In this century, usually the rebuke of elders is done in private, but because of this spirit and how it operates, that approach will not defeat it.

In confronting racism, there will always be excuses as to why promises that would demonstrate equality are not fulfilled. "We were unable to find candidates for the position"; "They were our second choice"; "We are working through the details"; and "Be patient; this is going to take some time" are all among common excuses that must be dismissed and addressed in order to move forward and continue to defeat this demonic spirit. Once these excuses are accepted, they will only further entrench and strengthen the spirit of racism while generating even more excuses such as, "We tried that before."

"Freedom is never voluntary given by the oppressor; it must be demanded by the oppressed." — Martin Luther King Jr. Letter from Birmingham Jail April 16, 1963

CHAPTER 3

Signs of Racism in the Church

> *"Our prayer must not be self-centered. It must arise not only because we feel our own need as a burden we must lay upon God, but also because we are so bound up in love for our fellow men that we feel their need as acutely as our own. To make intercession for men is the most powerful and practical way in which we can express our love for them." — John Calvin*

Acts 13:1 "Now there were in the church that was at Antioch certain prophets and teachers; as Barnabas, and Simeon that was called Niger, and Lucius of Cyrene, and Manaen, which had been brought up with Herod the tetrarch, and Saul."

These men were leaders in the Church at Antioch. Each of different ethnicities and socio-economic upbringings, yet we see them praying and sending Paul and Barnabas on their first missionary/Apostolic journey.

The church in America, and in many other parts of the world, is still segregated and lacks unity among the ethnic groups. In America, most metropolitan cities and urban areas where multitudes of ethnic groups dwell still have church congregations of primarily one ethnic group. This should be an obvious sign of racism within the core and foundations of the city that have infiltrated the Body of Christ. Not only should there be diversity within the leadership of local churches, but also there should be diversity within the city or community leadership, as well as with efforts such as food pantries, thrift stores and any para-church ministries within a geographical area. When one ethnic group is in control of all of these things, it sends the wrong message to the world.

When the principality of racism is in operation, the dominated culture tends to be angry, disenfranchised, distrustful and separated from and by the dominant culture. This only leads to disunity in the body of Christ.

Often, the dominant culture tends to believe it should and can minister to the dominated cultures and ethnicities but not incorporate those different ethnicities within their churches. Frequently, they create a separate church with a pastor of their own ethnicity and culture, while overseeing all aspects of the ministry, from finances to spiritual direction. Although accountability is needed in any ministry, lording over is not. We all need to understand that we have been grafted into the vine and our ethnicity, although important, is not primary. The dominate culture still wants to be in control and not allow the Holy Spirit to lead the newly formed congregation.

Incorporating other ethnic groups and cultures into any local church or denomination will require some work and some changes as to how a specific culture is injected in the church. If there is an overt amount of resistance to cultural changes, there may be racism in operation.

In Revelation 7:9, the Apostle John recounts,

> *"After this I beheld, and, lo, a great multitude, which no man could number, of all nations, and kindreds, and people, and tongues, stood before the throne, and before the Lamb, clothed with white robes, and palms in their hands;"*

In this account, he describes what he saw in in the throne room of heaven; every nation was together and language did not separate them. Culture did not separate them. Did this include the descendants of Ham? Of course it did; skin color did not separate them! Everyone had on the same white robes due to the blood of the Lamb that was slain before the foundations of the world!

Not believing that every ethnic group will be included leads to what I call "Give them a fish" instead of "Teach them to fish" mentality. This thinking or paradigm will always create dependency on the dominant culture and not dependence on God. This paradigm is to give them resources which will cause the ethnic group to depend on the dominate group instead of teaching them to create their own resources thereby depending on God.

In Matthew 6:10, Jesus prays to His Father, "Thy kingdom come. Thy will be done in earth, as *it is* in heaven." If churches and ministries are praying for

God's will to be done on earth, is it the expectation that they are seeking in Revelations 7:9, where all of God's people, regardless of color or ethnicity would worship together before the throne of God? Or, is the expectation something else? Is it to see all nations in one kingdom spreading the gospel throughout the earth together? Is it to see all ethnicities as equal partners in the kingdom? Or, is it something else?

I do understand cultural differences; however, cultural differences should not cause us to disregard our oneness in Christ. If a church is in a racially diverse area yet has no diversity within its leadership, that lack is an obvious sign of racism. I know there will be some diversity within the congregation, yet a lack of diversity within the leadership is unacceptable. And I am not referring to the praise and worship team and the dancers; people of color have historically been acknowledged for their singing and dancing. I am speaking of people of color in the leadership, working alongside the dominant culture, making decisions on what the church should be doing and the direction of its funds and resources.

People of color have been allowed to sing and dance for a while, now. Being on the praise and dance teams in and of itself is not wrong; being allowed to lead with and govern alongside the dominant group is the issue. Two thousand years ago at Antioch, there was diversity in the leadership, and because of it, God used Antioch to evangelize the known world. A little over 100 years ago, there was diversity at Azusa Street and the Holy Spirit used them to change the world!

Because of prophets and teachers, apostles were birthed out of Antioch, yet still today, there are barriers--or should I say a glass ceiling--for people of color in the church at large. Azusa Street birthed many of the Pentecostal/Charismatic denominations, yet we still have racism.

Let me say this: There are churches and denominations with predominantly one ethnicity that are doing great works in the kingdom, but we can do better.

Blindness

A sure sign of racism is blindness, which is a stronghold in the oppressor as well as in the oppressed. 2 Corinthians 10:4-5 teaches, "For the weapons of our warfare *are* not carnal, but mighty through God to the pulling down of strong holds; Casting down imaginations, and every high thing that exalteth itself against the knowledge of God, and bringing into captivity every thought to the obedience of Christ."

Strongholds are mental views and corresponding actions that, in an unregenerate mind, will continue to believe or do things that are against the Word of God. As racism unfolds in scripture, the Spirit of God addresses it and defeats it. A stronghold in one's mind is similar to a fortress. It is a belief we hold on to, defend, and will battle to keep, even if all the facts and evidence is to the contrary.

Maintaining the stronghold of racism has been defended overtly and, in many cases, with misapplied scripture. It has been defended with the unaware racism method of "Give them a fish". Just because an individual or church does not want to be racist does not mean that they are not. Many people who do not want to be racist are still racist; they just do not know it.

As noted in Acts 6 with the exclusion of the Greek widows, much emphasis is given to the deacons: how they were brought into existence, what their role was to be, etc. There is not much research given for this emphasis. The racial problem within the church and during a powerful release of the Holy Spirit that caused unfair treatment to Greek widows was solved because the first century believers agreed and submitted themselves to the Word of God through the Apostles. Therefore, we see that the church increased as well as the priests' obedience to the faith because all knew that every ethnicity would be treated fairly.

The reverse is happening in the Body of Christ today. When people of color bring racial injustice to the spiritual leaders of the dominant culture, for the most part, it is seen as complaining with little action taken. Many in the dominant culture even refuse to acknowledge that racism still exists. No one would ever think to tell the Jewish people to "just get over" the Holocaust; however, there seems to be a different story when it comes to reports of racism. Consequently, we see the church in America declining and many pastors and church leaders of all ethnicities leaving the ministry. We also see people of color separating themselves from the dominant church culture in just about every way, with a few exceptions.

A difference in styles of worship is often used as an excuse to exclude an ethnic group or force them to accept the dominant culture's style of music if there is to be fellowship. Yet, God can move with any culture's style of music.

I have been asked to participate in "joint" services with primarily European American congregations and there was no mention of styles or types of songs. When those same congregations were coming to our church, which was ethnically diverse, I was asked to make sure that we played worship songs that they knew, or should I say, "songs from their culture." This is subversive racism and is very offensive. First, it assumes that people of color do not enjoy the same songs as their European American counterparts. Then, it makes the assumption that whatever songs we play are of the African American culture or "gospel" and that those songs would not be considered in their churches. It also assumes that members of their church have never listened to or heard songs that we may play. How can you know who we are if you do not know how we worship? God can anoint music from all ethnicities. Perhaps the most insulting of it all is being asked to assimilate to that particular visiting culture, even at your own church, if you want to fellowship with them.

I perceive several things from this request: First, because I am an African American, the assumption is that the membership of our ministry is primarily people of color and therefore, has a different style of music that we should adjust to ensure the comfort of the visiting churches with the worship service. This question or concern was not raised when we went to their churches. The dominant group was not concerned whether we knew the songs or the words or not or if we were comfortable with the worship service.

Second, in America people of color are expected to adjust to the dominant church culture or we are viewed as a novelty, with the attitude, "That's the way *they* worship"--not quite as good as what we do but a novel or secondary way of worshiping God.

Racism is a very diverting and distracting spirit. It causes the people of God to focus on their differences instead of what God is doing in the earth. It causes the group that is being slighted or dominated to murmur and complain, and rightly so for the injustice. Yet, the Spirit and Power of God will step in and address this principality, given the right circumstances.

As in Acts 6, The Apostles did not blame the Greeks because the Jews were overlooking them. The Apostles did not guilt trip the Jews or act as though it was not important; they acknowledged that there was a disparity in the treatment of the Greek widows and offered a solution to the issue. It was obvious that there was a problem and the apostolic leaders implemented a solution that allowed the outpouring of the Holy Spirit, the continued study of the Word of God, and the move of God to continue.

> *Galatians 2:11-14 "But when Peter was come to Antioch, I withstood him to the face, because he was to be blamed. For before that certain came from James, he did eat with the Gentiles: but when they were come, he withdrew and separated himself, fearing them which were of the circumcision. And the other Jews dissembled likewise with him; insomuch that Barnabas also was carried away with their dissimulation. But when I saw that they walked not uprightly according to the truth of the gospel, I said unto Peter before them all, If thou, being a Jew, livest after the manner of Gentiles, and not as do the Jews, why compellest thou the Gentiles to live as do the Jews?"*

We see in this account that Peter was persuaded or was

fearful because of peer pressure from the dominant culture, his Jewish culture, which caused him to separate himself from Gentiles (non-Jews); this also drew Barnabas. This influence is powerful, even on men who should know better. The solution was that Paul confronted Peter face to face and wrote about it for all of history to recognize when it happens, even to those who are in leadership of a move of God. This pressure to discriminate cannot remain unchecked.

The same thing happened at Azusa! William Seymour, the son of a former slave, received a message concerning the power of the Holy Spirit from Charles Parham, and when Seymour opened the Azusa Street Church in 1906 with signs and wonders, the color line was erased. All ethnicities were included; black, white, brown and yellow prayed, ministered and worshipped together, much to the dismay of many whites who still could not deny the miracles signs and wonders. Yet the mixing of races, specifically of African American males and European American females, awoken the spirit of racism and caused many to oppose and discredit the church—with Charles Parham as one of the biggest detractors.

William Seymour's Leadership Team

Many of our leaders today and in America are being deceived and persuaded into believing that other ethnic groups are inferior in the church and that they are missing out on the anointing, revelation, and power that God has placed in that person. Even if that ethnic group or a person within that ethnic group demonstrates signs, wonders, and biblical proof that God is with them, the dominant culture will somehow, some way say that it is not of God or that it is not mainstream. This denial often turns many away from the very anointing and revelation that would set them free and allow them to break through.

We need strong leaders in this hour of the dominant culture to confront those who should know better and/or have perpetuated this spirit of racism so that the unity of the body of Christ can be restored and our attention returned to prayer and study of the Word. These leaders cannot be fearful that their culture will alienate them, which often means that funds dry up, but they must trust that God will sustain them as they battle the spirit of racism.

"We who engage in non-violent direct action are not the creators of tension. We merely bring to the surface the hidden tension that is already alive." — Martin Luther King Jr., Letter from Birmingham Jail April 16, 1963

CHAPTER 4

People of Color in the Bible

Acts 2:7-11 "And they were all amazed and marvelled, saying one to another, Behold, are not all these which speak Galileans? And how hear we every man in our own tongue, wherein we were born? Parthians, and Medes, and Elamites, and the dwellers in Mesopotamia, and in Judaea, and Cappadocia, in Pontus, and Asia, Phrygia, and Pamphylia, in Egypt, and in the parts of Libya about Cyrene, and strangers of Rome, Jews and proselytes, Cretes and Arabians, we do hear them speak in our tongues the wonderful works of God."

In his book, *Evidence of Black Africans in the Bible*, Dr. Dan Rodgers recalls,

"In 1992, I took a class at Emory University in Atlanta called 'Introduction to the Old Testament.' As I read the various required textbooks for the course, I saw something I had not noticed before. Many Old Testament scholars, particularly European scholars of the 18th, 19th and early 20th century, had written their books and commentaries on the Old Testament from the perspective that there were no people of color mentioned in the Scriptures.

Let me apologize in advance for some of the terms that I will need to use as we discuss this topic. They are not the terms we would prefer today, but they are terms that historians, ethnologists and Bible commentators of past centuries, and even the 20th century, have employed to explain their ideas about the origin of blacks. These ideas, steeped in racial prejudice, were alleged to provide a biblical justification for black slavery and the subjugation of black peoples.

When I first read about these concepts, they brought tears to my eyes. As a white person in a predominantly white country, I also began to gain a better understanding of and a greater appreciation for the black experience in the United States."

As Dr. Rodgers understood, just the very nature and location of events where the majority of the Bible takes place is in an area of Africa (Egypt) and the Middle East where there are mainly people of color. None of the Bible takes place in European nations, which is not to say descendants and mixtures of ethnic groups did not migrate to those areas. Hopefully, this dispels the depiction of Jesus Christ with straight blond hair and blue eyes, which is critical to the acceptance of other cultures in the body of Christ and His church.

Although there are many people of color throughout the Old and New Testaments, I would not try to identify them all. Instead, I will focus on five who are so intertwined in Christ that they warrant discussion.

Moses and his wife

Numbers 12:1 "And Miriam and Aaron spake against Moses because of the Ethiopian woman whom he had married: for he had married an Ethiopian woman."

A more accurate translation of Ethiopian is Cushite. Cushites were descendants of Ham whose descendants, as previously noted, were supposed to be cursed forever, and, according to Bible Study Tools.com, were thought to be a "generally a vile and contemptible race." Yet, one of Ham's descendants is married to Moses.

This does not sit well with his brother and sister. As the Lord spoke to the three of them, His response to Aaron and Miriam was obvious: the Bible makes note of the ethnicity of the woman, yet not her name! Also, I can only assume that Moses had love for his wife and she for him.

Reading further in Numbers, one can see that the Lord was not pleased with the response of Aaron and Miriam: "And the anger of the LORD was kindled against them; and he departed." Numbers 12:9

Simon of Cyrene

Matthew 27:32 "And as they came out, they found a man of Cyrene, Simon by name: him they compelled to bear his cross."

Simon of Cyrene became a believer in Jesus Christ and his sons were well known in the early church. He later travelled to Antioch and helped get the church there started. His wife and sons were with him. In

Antioch, he received the nickname *Niger,* "the black guy" for being a dark-skinned Jew. He was later joined in Antioch by Paul, then Saul of Tarsus, and later yet, John Mark, who both got to know and love him, his wife and sons. (Word Press)

Some dispute that this Simon is the one from Antioch. If he were not, then that would be an additional person of dark skin to be prominent in the early church. According to Galatians 3:13, "Christ hath redeemed us from the curse of the law, being made a curse for us: for it is written, Cursed *is* every one that hangeth on a tree." While this man Simon did not hang on that tree, he most assuredly carried the tree on which Christ hung.

Hagar and her son, Ishmael

Genesis 16:1 "Now Sarai Abram's wife bare him no children: and she had an handmaid, an Egyptian, whose name was Hagar."

Genesis 21:14, 17 "And Abraham rose up early in the morning, and took bread, and a bottle of water, and gave it unto Hagar, putting it on her shoulder, and the child, and sent her away: and she departed, and wandered in the wilderness of Beersheba. And God heard the voice of the lad; and the angel of God called to Hagar out of heaven, and said unto her, What aileth thee, Hagar? Fear not; for God hath heard the voice of the lad where he is."

H3458
yish-maw-ale'
From H8085 and H410; *God will hear; Jishmael, the*

name of Abraham's oldest son, and of five Israelites: - Ishmael.

> *Genesis 17:20 And as for Ishmael, I have heard thee: Behold, I have blessed him, and will make him fruitful, and will multiply him exceedingly; twelve princes shall he beget, and I will make him a great nation.*

So the son of an Egyptian handmaiden or servant would become a great nation also.

Ruth

Genealogy: the descent of David from Ruth

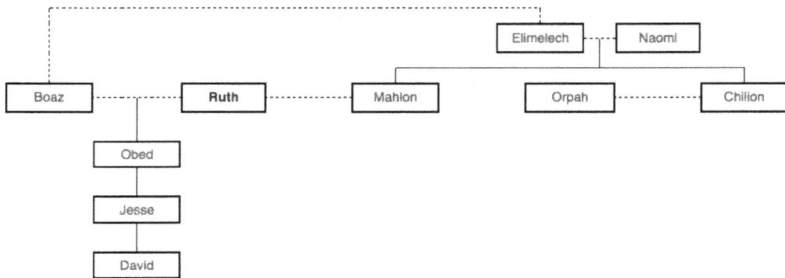

> *Ruth 1:16 "And Ruth said, Intreat me not to leave thee, or to return from following after thee: for whither thou goest, I will go; and where thou lodgest, I will lodge: thy people shall be my people, and thy God my God"*

We see that Ruth was the Great Grandmother of David King, Psalmist and Prophet of the nation of Israel.

Ethiopian Eunuch

Acts 8:26-27 "And the angel of the Lord spake unto Philip, saying, Arise, and go toward the south unto the way that goeth down from Jerusalem unto Gaza, which is desert.

And he arose and went: and, behold, a man of Ethiopia, an eunuch of great authority under Candace queen of the Ethiopians, who had the charge of all her treasure, and had come to Jerusalem for to worship."

While the Book of Acts does not give the Eunuch's name specifically, it does give his ethnicity. From this account, we can discern that he was sent by Queen Candace and that he was in charge of the treasury. Most importantly, however, he had a copy of the prophets, which means he and his people were aware of Jehovah God. His purpose for traveling to Jerusalem was to worship or to give tithes and offerings. God knew exactly where he was and what he needed.

God has always included all ethnicities in his plan of redemption from the beginning of calling Abram out of a people. He will continue to do so in this age.

CHAPTER 5

Where Do We Go From Here?

2 Corinthians 10:4-6 "For the weapons of our warfare are not carnal, but mighty through God to the pulling down of strong holds; Casting down imaginations, and every high thing that exalteth itself against the knowledge of God, and bringing into captivity every thought to the obedience of Christ; And having in a readiness to revenge all disobedience, when your obedience is fulfilled."

"Sir, my concern is not whether God is on our side; my greatest concern is to be on God's side, for God is always right." — Abraham Lincoln

In order for the majority of what I am about to say be effective, there needs to be a dramatic paradigm shift from "individuals" and "churches" to "Body of Christ" and "Kingdom." I am not saying that individuals and specific churches are not important; only, they are not the *most* important. Jesus taught in Matthew 6:33, "But seek ye first the kingdom of God, and his righteousness; and all these things shall be added unto you." If we understand that the bulk of the New Testament, specifically Apostle Paul's letters, with the exception of 1st and 2nd Timothy and Titus, were written not to one church, but to churches in the city or region, then we can begin to understand how Christ taught and manifested the Kingdom of God.

We must be more concerned about the health of the church at large in a city or region as we gauge the impact that the body of Christ has on it. Luke 11:17 states that, "But he, knowing their thoughts, said unto them, Every kingdom divided against itself is brought to desolation; and a house *divided* against a house falleth." We have convinced ourselves that this present state of racial dysfunction is a "united" Kingdom of God. We have seen mega churches arise of predominantly one ethnic group and have accepted this as the standard instead of true unity among all the tribes of God. When will we face reality and understand we need each other in order for the Kingdom of God, not our own kingdoms, to arise and cover the earth? It is obvious that there can be many churches, even mega churches in a city or region, yet that does not a guarantee that the byproducts of God's Kingdom are manifesting themselves.

Romans 14:17 "For the kingdom of God is not meat and drink; but righteousness, and peace, and joy in the Holy Ghost." When the church of Jesus Christ is fully manifesting the Kingdom, then,

- Righteousness will be the dominant characteristic within all aspects of the region: government, education, law enforcement and businesses.

- There will be <u>peace</u> among <u>all</u> the people; crime, violence and drugs will be at a minimum. The initial major battle against the devil will be won and only minor flare-ups will happen.

- <u>Joy</u> and optimism will be throughout the region. The needs of all who are in want will be met and brotherly love will abound.

God's desire is not to have just a church or group of churches that prosper but the entire city. Even the unsaved should see the difference and support the need for the church in the region. If this occurs, even though not everyone may receive salvation, everyone will respect the authority and impact that the church has on the city.

As with most demonic strongholds, they have resided in families, cities, ethnic groups, and even countries for generations, even centuries. In addition, just like spirits of divorce and lust, these principalities gain strength the longer they are in control. The best course of action must be joint efforts. Although dialogues and forums on racism are helpful, unless the church in a city or region receives and then offers deliverance, there will be only limited and/or short-lived successes.

Most people in America realize the disparities between the ethnic groups; for those who do not acknowledge that there is a disparity in your church, this is the first place to start. Because the church is the only institution that has the power to break this spirit's hold on a church, city or region, we must take the lead in the majority of race-related issues. For church leaders and lay members to oppose efforts to confront racism is a confirmation that racism is present.

In any effort to pull down any stronghold, there must be a starting point. It can be a church or group of churches, but the most effective place would be with the church leaders or with the gatekeeper of a city or region. If you are not familiar with spiritual mapping, it would be good to study your region before you devise a strategy.

Regional leaders must face and address any area of racism, overt or unaware, within the body of Christ, in order for their respective congregations to receive ministry. Are we willing to pool our assets and distribute them to the churches in need? Are we willing to make sure that every church ordained by God has what it needs to reach the people to whom it has been called?

What Is Spiritual Mapping?

It is an attempt to see our region as it really is and not as it appears to be (George Otis Jnr.). He also says it is the discipline of diagnosing the obstacles to revival in a given community through fervent prayer and diligent research.

Spiritual Mapping is not an end in itself- it is a means to an end.

- It is not demon hunting or searching for names of demons, although the Holy Spirit will reveal names and /or identities where He feels we need to know.
- It is not a one-person task, but teamwork.
- It is not about learning a lot of principals and carrying them out, but about doing the God appointed thing for your city.
- It is not the only way that God works in transforming

the city, but it is a major component.

- It is not conclusions based on inadequate investigations. It must be done properly.
- It is not spiritual warfare, but a preparation for it.

Once there is adequate prayer and preparation, before you go out and do anything, check your hearts for any unaware racism. There will come a time when the Kingdom of God confronts the kingdom of darkness. Although it may seem like natural circumstances, do not be fooled by what you see. Remember pulling down the principality of racism is just the means to an end of God's Kingdom coming and His will being done.

Within the churches in a community, city or region there must be apostolic/pastoral leaders who are willing to fellowship and worship together, to model the transition into equity. This may not be an easy transition and each church will need much ministry.

As we learned with the Greeks and the Hebrews, in a specific city or region, the dominant ethnic group cannot and should not continue to ignore other ethnic groups' needs to create a successful ministry in their area of influence. The dominant ethnic group should not believe that it is alright or God's will that the majority of the resources and finances be controlled and contained in their denomination or churches. Instead, they should understand that, like in Acts 6, if all God-ordained churches and their congregations are supplied with the necessary funds and resources, then, as in Acts 6:7, "The word of God increased; and the number of the disciples multiplied in Jerusalem greatly; and a great company of the priests were obedient to the faith."

Remember this was a city-wide decree from the apostles! There must be men and women chosen to determine how the "daily ministration" is to be distributed within a city or region.

The fact that priests became obedient to the faith, means that some priests were not obeying the Word of God. Even now, some ministers (priests) may not be true to the Word of God.

Resources include equipment and finances, but most importantly people. White privilege also operates within churches as they interact with banks and financial institutions, contractors, accountants and other needed secular non-church related businesses. In order for all to be successful, these resources must be equally available to all.

For one church to have millions of dollars in savings and another God-ordained church to not have enough to supply basic needs to survive should never happen in the body of Christ. Within that city or region, there must be godly interaction between churches by the active sharing of resources. Often, it is embarrassing and/or humiliating for people of color to receive from or ask for help from the dominant culture, but humility on all sides is what is needed to break racism's hold on finances and resources in a region.

In America, our success is gauged by what we have materially instead of spiritually. We must break free of this mindset and understand what standards of success God presents in His Word. Then, we must be willing to share that success, whether financial or spiritual, with those to whom God has called us.

The Cornelius Connections

Acts 10:1-23 "There was a certain man in Caesarea called Cornelius, a centurion of the band called the Italian band, A devout man, and one that feared God with all his house, which gave much alms to the people, and prayed to God alway.

He saw in a vision evidently about the ninth hour of the day an angel of God coming in to him, and saying unto him, Cornelius.

And when he looked on him, he was afraid, and said, What is it, Lord? And he said unto him, Thy prayers and thine alms are come up for a memorial before God.

And now send men to Joppa, and call for one Simon, whose surname is Peter: He lodgeth with one Simon a tanner, whose house is by the sea side: he shall tell thee what thou oughtest to do.

And when the angel which spake unto Cornelius was departed, he called two of his household servants, and a devout soldier of them that waited on him continually; And when he had declared all these things unto them, he sent them to Joppa.

On the morrow, as they went on their journey, and drew nigh unto the city, Peter went up upon the housetop to pray about the sixth hour: And he became very hungry, and would have eaten: but while they made ready, he fell into a trance, And saw heaven opened, and a certain vessel descending unto him, as it had been a great sheet knit at the four corners, and let down to the earth: Wherein were all manner of fourfooted beasts of the earth, and wild beasts, and creeping things, and fowls of the air.

And there came a voice to him, Rise, Peter; kill, and eat. But Peter said, Not so, Lord; for I have never eaten any thing that is common or unclean. And the voice spake unto him again the second time, What God hath cleansed, that call not thou common. This was done thrice: and the vessel was received up again into heaven.

Now while Peter doubted in himself what this vision which he had seen should mean, behold, the men which were sent from Cornelius had made enquiry for Simon's house, and stood before the gate, And called, and asked whether Simon, which was surnamed Peter, were lodged there.

While Peter thought on the vision, the Spirit said unto him, Behold, three men seek thee. Arise therefore, and get thee down, and go with them, doubting nothing: for I have sent them.

Then Peter went down to the men which were sent unto him from Cornelius; and said, Behold, I am he whom ye seek: what is the cause wherefore ye are come? And they said, Cornelius the centurion, a just man, and one that feareth God, and of good report among all the nation of the Jews, was warned from God

*by an holy angel to send for thee into his house,
and to hear words of thee.*

*Then called he them in, and lodged them. And
on the morrow Peter went away with them, and
certain brethren from Joppa accompanied him."*

In this account, the Holy Spirit first spoke to Cornelius
but then had to speak to Peter three times in order to
get him to move past his ethnic traditions that would
cause him to reject Cornelius. Peter called these things
unclean and God's response was do not call things
common which I have cleansed!

I believe that God is preparing the hearts of both
the dominated groups and the dominant group into
relationships that will further the kingdom of God;
these are Cornelius connections. Both groups must
be willing to answer the call of God to work together,
regardless of what has happened in the past, to bring
a new future into the earth realm and to those directly
associated with the things of God.

Many times, it will take supernatural visitations to
convince those who have been blinded by unaware
racism to have the courage to cross racial, cultural
and ethnic barriers in order to expand the Kingdom of
God. With the possibility of offending and alienating
their own ethnic group or denomination, this will take
some courage on both sides.

This is one of the best ways to help any ministry
grow. A visit from a prominent, internationally known
minister to a conference, without expecting over-the-
top compensation, could be just the thing a growing
ministry needs to fulfill its call. It could provide

recognition and validation of what God is doing. But most of all, it could serve as affirmation to that ministry and the leadership team that the Cornelius Connection was of God and everyone involved obeyed the voice of God.

Intercession

1 Timothy 2:1-3 "I exhort therefore, that, first of all, supplications, prayers, intercessions, and giving of thanks, be made for all men; For kings, and for all that are in authority; that we may lead a quiet and peaceable life in all godliness and honesty. For this is good and acceptable in the sight of God our Saviour."

As churches and people become more and more aware of this principality of racism, there must be strong intercession in order to dismantle the principality. Intercessors must offer supplication, prayers, intercessions and thanksgiving for leaders in these institutions. First, intercessors must pray for the leaders of the church of Jesus Christ. The leaders in the church must develop the courage to continue the spiritual warfare necessary in order to confront the institutions within their own churches and denomination that are giving strength to this principality. This comes by prayer and fasting.

Obvious leaders to pray for within the region are the mayor, council members, school superintendents, police and fire chiefs, making sure that those in charge of human resources and anyone involved in hiring is included by name. Also, identify any board members or other groups that may have major influence in city, community or region and intercede for them also.

This focused prayer must be done regardless of denominational affiliation, political affiliation or ethnicity. Remember: the goal is to defeat the spirit of racism within these institutions. The purpose is not to promote any political party or denomination but the Kingdom of God. **Conclusion: Forgiveness is the Key**

> *Romans 3:23 "For all have sinned, and come short of the glory of God." (KJV)*

If the Body of Christ continues to ignore racism and say things like "Just get over it," or "That happened years ago," the forces of darkness will continue to limit what really could happen in the Kingdom of God. We must forgive one another, stop shifting blame and own up to the atrocities that we, as well as our ancestors, have done to one another and have true repentance and reconciliation among the races. Empty ceremonies have not worked, and the ethnic group in power is still in power.

In the Old Testament, each tribe in the nation of Israel was valued because of what they brought to the fulfillment of the whole. Israel and Esau forgave each other and the one with the most, Esau, gave to his Brother, Israel.

King David wrote in Psalms 133:1-3, "Behold, how good and how pleasant *it is* for brethren to dwell together in unity! *It is* like the precious ointment upon the head that ran down upon the beard, *even* Aaron's beard: that went down to the skirts of his garments; As the dew of Hermon, *and as the dew* that descended upon the mountains of Zion: for there the LORD commanded the blessing, *even* life for evermore."

This psalm, in the context of the brethren, was referring to the 12 tribes of Israel, not just one tribe, but to <u>all</u> the tribes. Likewise, we should understand that the full blessings of God are much more than we could ever imagine if the body of Christ defeated the principality of racism. White unity, black unity, brown unity, yellow unity and red unity are good, but they are still dwelling separately in disunity of the whole.

With the racial tensions happening in Europe, Africa and in America, it should be obvious to all who are not under the influence of this spirit that the conversation on race and race relations is still necessary. Will the Church of Jesus Christ be at the forefront of overcoming the principality of racism or just another footnote in the history of the earth? I believe that if the body of Christ would come together and defeat this spirit, we would see what has happened every time the whole body of Christ, regardless of ethnicity, has come together under the banner of Jesus Christ.

When revival breaks out, all ethnicities are drawn from the uttermost parts of the earth to worship the King of kings and Lord of lords. The color line that divides us will be erased as our focus returns to Christ and His Kingdom. If not, will we need to wait another 100 years to experience the power and presence of God that was at the day of Pentecost or at Azusa? Will dominant cultures around the world be willing to give up power, prestige and resources to restore what their ancestors and fellow ethnic group members have stolen, taken or dominated? Are power, prestige and ethnic pride more important than God revealing Himself to His creation in a supernatural way? Will dominated cultures be able to forgive the atrocities and accept the repented apologies of those who have offended? Only time will tell. One thing is certain: it will get better or it will get much worse. The choice is ours.

John 10:10 "The thief cometh not, but for to steal, and to kill, and to destroy: I am come that they might have life, and that they might have it more abundantly."

Discussion Questions

1. Do you believe that racism is affecting The Church in America?

2. If it is, what are some action steps to dismantle racism?

3. If not, explain why not?

4. Why is racism, for the most part, not preached about from our pulpits?

5. Is your church racially diverse? If so why, if not why not?

To keep the conversation open you can post your answers to these and other questions in my blog at:

ronjamesministries.com

Bibliography

Cauchi, Tony. "Arthur Osterberg, Oral History of the Azusa Street Revival." *William J. Seymour and the Origins of Global Pentecostalism A Biography and Documentary History* (2014): 319-20. Web.

"Charles Fox Parham." *Wikipedia*. Wikimedia Foundation, n.d. Web. 6 August. 2015. https:// en.m.wikipedia.org/wiki/Charles_Fox_Parham>.

"Cultural Assimilation." *Wikipedia*. Wikimedia Foundation, n.d. Web. 6 August. 2015. <https:// en.wikipedia.org/wiki/Cultural_assimilation>.

"Definitions of Racism." *Definitions of Racism*. New York, NY: Council on Interracial for Children, 1986. N. pag. Web.

"Discrimination." *Wikipedia*. Wikimedia Foundation, n.d. Web. 6 August. 2015. <https://en.wikipedia.org/ wiki/Discrimination>.

Ham, Ken. "Interracial Marriage: Is It Biblical?" *Creation*, 1999, 21(3):22-25.

"Institutionalized Racism." *Wikipedia*. Wikimedia Foundation, n.d. Web. 6 August. 2015. <https://en.wikipedia.org/wiki/Institutional_racism>.

King, Jr., Martin Luther. Where Do We Go from Here: Chaos or Community? New York: Harper & Row, 1967. Print.

"Male Privilege." *Wikipedia*. Wikimedia Foundation, n.d. Web. 6 August. 2015. <https://en.wikipedia.org/wiki/Male_privelege>.

"Prejudice." *Wikipedia*. Wikimedia Foundation, n.d. Web. 6 August. 2015. <https://en.wikipedia.org/wiki/Prejudice>.

"Racism." *Merriam-Webster*. Merriam-Webster, n.d. Web. 25 Nov. 2015. <http://www.merriam-webster.com/>.

"Racism." *Oxford Dictionaries - Dictionary, Thesaurus, & Grammar*. N.p., n.d. Web. 11 August. 2015. <http://www.oxforddictionaries.com/>.

"Racism." *Wikipedia*. Wikimedia Foundation, n.d. Web. 6 August. 2015. <https://en.wikipedia.org/wiki/Racism>.

Robeck, Cecil M. *A Pentecostal Perpective on Leadership*. N.p.: n.p., n.d. N. pag. Print. Rogers, Dr. Dan. "Grace Communion International." *Evidence of Black Africans in the Bible*. N.p., n.d. Web. 15 Nov. 2015. <https://www.gci.org/bible/africans>.

www.ingramcontent.com/pod-product-compliance
Lightning Source LLC
Chambersburg PA
CBHW071632040426
42452CB00009B/1582